SPACE SYSTEMS

The Composition of the Universe
The Evolution of Stars and Galaxies

Rachel Keranen

Cavendish
Square

New York

Published in 2017 by Cavendish Square Publishing, LLC
243 5th Avenue, Suite 136, New York, NY 10016

Copyright © 2017 by Cavendish Square Publishing, LLC

First Edition

Library of Congress Cataloging-in-Publication Data

Names: Keranen, Rachel.
Title: The composition of the universe : the evolution of stars and galaxies / Rachel Keranen.
Description: New York : Cavendish Square Publishing, [2017] | Series: Space systems | Includes bibliographical references and index.
Identifiers: LCCN 2016022615 (print) | LCCN 2016025087 (ebook) | ISBN 9781502622853 (library bound) | ISBN 9781502622860 (E-book)
Subjects: LCSH: Stars--Evolution--Juvenile literature. | Galaxies--Evolution--Juvenile literature. | Astronomy--History--Juvenile literature. | Cosmology--Juvenile literature.
Classification: LCC QB806 .K47 2017 (print) | LCC QB806 (ebook) | DDC 523.1/12--dc23

LC record available at https://lccn.loc.gov/2016022615

Editorial Director: David McNamara
Editor: Caitlyn Miller
Copy Editor: Rebecca Rohan
Associate Art Director: Amy Greenan
Designer: Alan Sliwinski
Production Assistant: Karol Szymczuk
Photo Research: J8 Media

Contents

The universe is composed of stars, galaxies, gas, and dust, and massive amounts of mysterious matter we cannot see.

Introduction: A Beautiful Universe

"They cannot scare me with their empty spaces
Between stars—on stars where no human race is.
I have it in me so much nearer home
To scare myself with my own desert places."
—Robert Frost

Beyond Earth, beyond the solar system, there is a great and wonderful universe. Most of the universe is emptier than the strongest vacuums on Earth, but it is not entirely empty. Amid all that near-emptiness, there are phenomena bigger and more powerful than anything we see in our daily lives: stars forming, stars dying, gas clouds forming, **black holes** ejecting massive jets of gas and light, and galaxies colliding and merging with one another.

Before telescopes existed, our understanding of the universe was limited to what we could observe with the naked eye. A desire for a neatly ordered, human-centered universe led early scientists like Aristotle down the wrong path, hypothesizing a universe with Earth at the center, surrounded by nested spheres that held the moon, the sun, and the stars. A shift toward observation during the Scientific Revolution revealed that Earth was not the center of the universe. As instrumentation improved, it became progressively more clear that there were other planets, that the stars moved in their own paths, and, eventually, that we lived in a **galaxy** that was just one of many.

Modern astronomy took off full force in the early twentieth century. Albert Einstein shook the scientific world with his theories of general relativity. General relativity changed the way we understood gravity and predicted many new mysterious forces in the universe. Around the same time, Edwin Hubble used the world's biggest telescope (at the time) to observe the movement of galaxies away from us. The universe, he realized, is expanding.

Close observations of galaxies showed that galaxy dynamics didn't make sense given the amount of known mass, leading to the discovery of invisible **dark matter** that outnumbers ordinary matter by about six times. Dark matter, we learned, shapes not just the orbit and velocity of galaxies, but the very formation of those galaxies in the early days of the universe. Dark matter encourages the growth of structure through its gravitational effects, while another component of the universe, **dark energy,** drives those structures away from each other at an accelerating rate.

Within the galaxies, stars grow from clouds of gas and dust, shine brilliantly, and die stunning deaths. The smaller stars like our sun release planetary **nebulae** and fade into retirement as white dwarves. Heavier stars die in brilliant **supernova** explosions and become small, dense **neutron stars,** while the heaviest stars become the densest thing we know: black holes. Nothing escapes once it crosses the **event horizon** of a black hole, including light and information, so there is little known about their inner workings.

Many minds and many instruments have been essential to uncovering our current understanding of the universe. In addition to Albert Einstein and Edwin Hubble, we have the work of Henrietta Swan Leavitt, who pioneered a technique that Hubble and others used to calculate distance, and J. Robert Oppenheimer, who theorized on the formation of black holes before leading the Manhattan Project.

Telescopes grew increasingly large, with bigger and bigger mirrors that could capture more light and thus see deeper into space. We kept some of these giant telescopes on Earth; others we shot into space to look at the universe from beyond the haze of Earth's atmosphere. The Hubble Space Telescope showed us beautiful images of galaxies, while satellites like

COBE, WMAP, and Planck showed us what the young universe was like before it gave birth to galaxies and the structures we see today. From these images, we learned more about how these galaxies first formed and how stars are born and die within them.

Astrophysicists are not like other physicists who can conduct their experiments in a lab. Astrophysicists' objects of study are too large to recreate here on Earth. Modern computing and the power of parallel programming have allowed for virtual labs, in which scientists visualize the evolution of the universe and the structure of galaxies in stunning computer simulations. They enter the laws of physics as we know them into a computer program, add particles of matter, and see what happens. If the simulation produces a universe, a galaxy, a black hole like we see in observations, scientists are on the right track. When the simulations reveal discrepancies, there is work to do.

Ongoing research focuses on the mysterious aspects of black holes, **quasars**, dark matter, and dark energy. So much of what shapes the composition and evolution of our universe is invisible or very difficult to see.

Even our current understanding of cosmology, which observations of the early universe and computer simulations validate, is still a theory. The scientific method requires rigorous testing and the willingness to walk away from a theory that testing proves to be false. Science requires us to seek better and better understandings of the universe we observe. Above all else, it is important to keep an open and curious mind, to evaluate evidence critically, and to continually seek to further existing knowledge and make new discoveries.

Some of the theories discussed in this book, such as the life cycle of stars, have been part of our accepted cosmology for quite some time. Others, such as the expansion of the universe and acceleration of distant galaxies away from us, are predicated on newer discoveries. As you read, understand that new information will continue to shape the way we understand our universe and the evolution of stars and galaxies.

Ancient Greek philosophers believed the universe was structured like nested spheres, with Earth at the center.

Early
Predictions

B efore the advent of telescopes, knowledge of the universe
beyond our own planet was severely limited. Very little
was known about the movement, much less the life cycle, of
stars. Galaxies were unknown.

ANCIENT BELIEFS

Early cultures intertwined the sun, moon, and stars into their
mythologies, associating the movement of celestial bodies
with events on Earth. Ancient Egyptians, for example,
tracked the star Sirius, whose disappearance and subsequent
reappearance near the summer solstice marked the beginning
of flood season. In another example, Stonehenge and other
stone circles in Great Britain are thought to have been
prehistoric temples built to align with the movements of
the sun. And yet, while many ancient cultures tracked the

movements of the sun and other stars, knowledge of the universe was limited by the lack of technology.

The ancient Greeks began to take a scientific approach to cosmology, but philosophy often stood in the way of accuracy. Greek philosopher Aristotle, born in 384 BCE, put forth a popular and long-lasting model of a perfect and unchanging universe made of crystalline nesting spheres. In the Aristotelian model, Earth stood stationary at the center of the universe. The moon, planets, sun, and stars moved in rotating, concentric spheres between Earth and the sphere of the divine. Aristotle's model was beautiful, but it failed to align with actual observations of celestial movement.

(Aristotle did predict that the Milky Way's bright band of stars in the night sky was the result of numerous stars close together, but he fit this idea into his model.)

The Greek mathematician Ptolemy, born around 100 CE, attempted to make the basis of Aristotle's model more consistent with observed celestial motion by adding concepts called the deferent and equant to more closely model the observed planetary motion. Ptolemy's model was by and large accepted until the Scientific Revolution over a thousand years later.

THE SCIENTIFIC REVOLUTION

The Scientific Revolution, which emerged in Europe after the Middle Ages and extended roughly between 1500 and 1700, brought about new technology and massive changes in how scientists and nonscientists alike thought about the universe.

Copernicus Proposes a Heliocentric Model of the Universe

In 1543, Copernicus proposed a model of the universe with a stationary sun at the center of moving, rotating planets. He placed the planets in the order we know today, with Earth third from the Sun after Mercury and Venus.

Copernicus's system was groundbreaking because it challenged centuries of established thought. Earth was no longer in an exalted, central, fixed position, but instead an imperfect and changing body moving through the heavens along with many other planets. However, Copernicus still maintained the circular celestial movements of previous systems.

Brahe and Kepler

The observations of Danish astronomer Tycho Brahe helped bring about the next advancements in astronomy, both in his own work and that of his assistant Johannes Kepler. In 1572, a few decades after Copernicus published his heliocentric theory, Brahe thought that he discovered a bright new star in the constellation Cassiopeia. We know now that what Brahe actually observed was a supernova, or an exploding star shining with a **luminosity** (a brightness) of up to 10 billion suns. Though he mistook the death of a star for the birth of a star, his observations forced scientists to make new models that accounted for evolving stars.

(As an indicator of the state of astronomy before telescopes, Brahe's supernova was one of just seven supernovas known to have been recorded before the seventeenth century. Today, we know that the Milky Way galaxy alone has a supernova explosion about every fifty years on average.)

Brahe made comprehensive astronomical observations over his lifetime, including deep study of the solar system and the positions of almost 800 stars. He recorded positions every day and night possible for years. After Brahe's death, and after some political struggle over who owned Brahe's intellectual property, his assistant Johannes Kepler took Brahe's data.

A few years after Brahe's death, Kepler published his first law of planetary motion, showing that planets move in an elliptical (not circular) orbit around the sun. Kepler's work turned Copernicus's neat circular model into a more chaotic, dynamic universe. In finding new answers, he created many new questions and paved the way for future physicists such as Newton and Einstein.

Newtonian Gravity

English physicist and astronomer Isaac Newton contributed a significant amount to astronomy with his theory of gravity. Early astronomers and physicists including Kepler knew that the planets orbited the sun, but they didn't know what forces kept them in orbit. Newton, born in 1642, was the first to suggest that the force in question is gravity.

Gravity operates on large bodies like stars and galaxies, on the objects of our daily lives, and on the small particles of gas and dust in outer space. The force of gravity holds our solar system and galaxy together. Gravity also determines the escape velocity of an object: the stronger gravity is, the faster an object must travel to escape its pull.

According to Newton, any two objects in the universe exert gravitational attraction on one another based on the mass of the objects and how far apart they are. Larger masses create a stronger gravitational attraction, and greater distances weaken the effects of gravity.

TELESCOPES ADVANCE EARLY UNDERSTANDINGS OF THE UNIVERSE

Even as fundamental shifts in astronomy were underway during the Scientific Revolution, scientists understood very little about the evolution of stars and galaxies. They were simply too far away to study with any detail or accuracy. Then in 1608, Dutch eyeglass maker Hans Lippershey was the first person to apply for a telescope patent. Lippershey's design involved a tube placed between a concave glass eyepiece and a convex glass lens that magnified objects by three times.

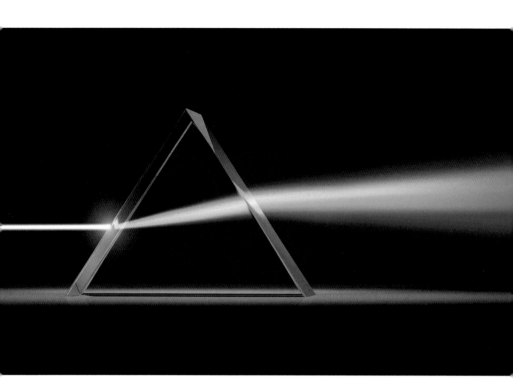

Wavelengths of light travel at the same speed through a vacuum but at different speeds when passing through glass.

Isaac Newton built the world's first reflecting telescope, which markedly changed the path of telescope design, and changed the way scientists thought about light, an important concept and tool in studying stars and galaxies, as well as other parts of the universe. Previously, the long-held belief was that light was a pure substance and phenomena like rainbows occurred due to modification of the light itself. Newton conducted experiments casting light spectra on dark walls and proposed that resulting rainbows of light were not a modification of the light but a natural result of rays within light that behave differently from one another. He suggested that different rays of light refract at different angles, and that glass lenses would always produce distortion as different rays of light failed to come into a unified focus.

To counter that effect, in 1668, Newton built a telescope that relied on a mirror to reflect light instead of refracting it. The light does not disperse, so the focus was improved compared to the previous style of refracting telescopes. Today's telescopes are also predominantly reflecting telescopes that rely on mirrors.

Herschel's Cosmology

In 1784, a German musician and amateur astronomer living in England named William Herschel made his own mirrors and telescopes, eventually casting and shaping such fine mirrors that he had telescopes that were better than those used at the Greenwich Observatory. Using his telescopes, Herschel and his sister Caroline mapped the distribution of stars and nebulae, discovered the planet Uranus, and attempted to make a map of the Milky Way. Herschel's map correctly showed that our galaxy was a disk, but he placed our sun at the center. (It's not.)

Herschel's expansive surveys of the sky and his work on nebulae prompted him to propose one of the first theories of star and galaxy evolution. Many astronomers thought the nebulae, or luminous patches of light in the sky, were made

The First Salaried Female Astronomer

Caroline Herschel, William Herschel's sister, was born in 1750 in Hanover, Germany. While her brothers were educated in mathematics, music, and other disciplines, and her father wanted the same for Caroline, Caroline's mother didn't believe a girl needed an education. Her mother forced her to focus on basic housework, and Caroline received education from her father only when her mother was away.

At age twenty-two, Caroline moved to Bath, England, to serve as a housekeeper for William, who was a musician and growing astronomy enthusiast. Caroline not only recorded his observations and helped him build his telescopes, she also became a dedicated observer of the night sky herself. Caroline created a catalogue of stars and a catalogue of all the nebulae they discovered. She herself discovered eleven nebulae and clusters in 1783 and two more in 1784 and 1787, respectively. Two of these objects later turned out to be galaxies. Caroline made these discoveries with a relatively small telescope, which showed how numerous nebulae were in the universe. This prompted William to pivot his focus onto nebulae surveys. She also found eight comets between 1786 and 1797.

When William married at forty-nine, he no longer needed Caroline as a housekeeper, and she moved out. He offered her money, but she preferred a different solution. Herschel had been named astronomer to King George III, and Caroline asked to be listed as his assistant and given a salary from the king. The king approved, making Caroline the first salaried female astronomer in history.

Late in life, Caroline received the King of Prussia's Gold Medal of Science for her work. She died in 1848.

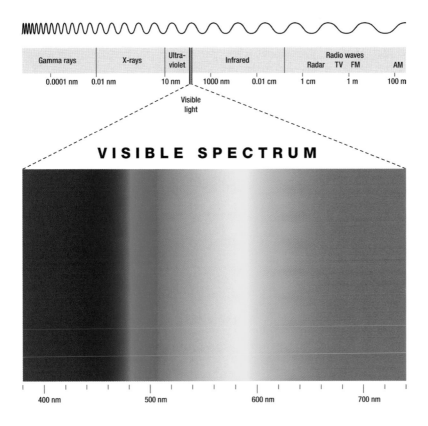

VISIBLE SPECTRUM

400 nm	500 nm	600 nm	700 nm	

Gamma rays | X-rays | Ultra-violet | Infrared | Radio waves — Radar TV FM — AM

0.0001 nm   0.01 nm   10 nm   1000 nm   0.01 cm   1 cm   1 m   100 m

Visible light

We can't see most of the electromagnetic spectrum, but we do experience other portions in daily life, including radio waves.

of some unknown milky substance. With his telescopes, Herschel could see that several nebulae were actually made of individual stars. (Today we call the "nebulae" that Herschel observed **galaxies**, systems of stars held together by gravity. Nebulae, or clouds of gas and dust, do exist within galaxies, but galaxies are not a type of nebula.) Nebulae that remained fuzzy must be further off, he predicted, and must be huge systems of stars.

Herschel hypothesized that the universe had begun with stars scattered across infinite space that, due to attractive forces, eventually fragmented into separate clusters. Clusters with more scattered stars were younger, Herschel thought, and hadn't had as much time to pull together.

Herschel made significant discoveries in several other areas as well. He documented 848 pairs of **binary stars**, which he called "double stars," and was the first to show through careful measurements that binary stars orbit one another.

He was also the first to discover infrared rays and show that there was light beyond the visible spectrum. To do so, he used a glass prism to create a spectrum of light and measured the temperature of the different colors with a blackened thermometer (which absorbed heat better). He noticed that the temperature of the light increased from the blue end to the red end of the spectrum. He measured the temperature to the right of the red end of the spectrum, where no visible light appeared, and found the temperature was even higher. He had discovered the infrared portion of the electromagnetic spectrum and shown that there is light we cannot see. Astrophysicists now study the cosmos using many invisible parts of the electromagnetic spectrum, including infrared radiation as well as gamma rays and ultraviolet (UV) radiation.

MODERN PREDICTIONS AND PROGRESS

In the twentieth century, the close study of stars and galaxies took off. With better telescopes and understandings of light spectra and physics, scientists were more equipped to study wide swaths of the far-off regions of the universe and create theories of star and galaxy evolution.

Einstein's Gravity

Albert Einstein amended Newton's theory of gravity with his general theory of relativity. According to Einstein, gravity is the result of distortions in space and time (or, as the unification of space and time is called, space-time). Imagine a trampoline with a bowling ball in the center. The surface of the trampoline represents space-time; the bowling ball represents an object such as a star. If you place a marble on the same trampoline, it will roll toward the bowling ball due to the curvature of the surface. In Einstein's theory, the bowling ball is not exerting an attractive force that acts on the marble—the bowling ball warps space-time, and the marble moves along that curvature. Another way to understand Einstein's theory of gravity is in the words of physicist John Wheeler: "Matter tells space-time how to curve, and curved space-time tells matter how to move."

The Hooker Telescope's massive glass disk reflects light to a photographic plate placed over 42 feet (12.8 m) away.

The Composition of the Universe: The Evolution of Stars and Galaxies

Notably, Einstein also posited that gravity affects the path of light, which has since been observed to be true. Because light is energy and not mass, in Newton's equation gravity would not affect light. In Einstein's theory, however, light typically follows a straight line path that curves when the space-time it's traversing is curved due to gravity. A team of scientists proved this was true in 1919 by observing how starlight bent when it traveled near the sun.

An Ever Bigger Universe

In the early twentieth century, at the Mount Wilson Observatory in Pasadena, California, American astronomer Harlow Shapley discovered that the sun was not at the center of our galaxy. Shapley estimated that the sun was actually located in the galactic disk, some 50,000 light years from the center. (We now know that the sun is about 25,000 light years from the center.)

Like most scientists of his time, Shapley mistakenly believed that the spiral "nebulae" he saw in the sky were clouds of gas in the Milky Way. The prevailing thought was that the Milky Way was the only galaxy and that all things were contained within it. Some believed these spiral nebulae were simply new solar systems forming.

In the early 1920s, American astronomer Edwin Hubble also worked at Mount Wilson Observatory, which at the time had the world's largest telescope, the Hooker telescope.

The Andromeda Nebula

(Having the largest telescope was a serious advantage for studying far-off regions and times in the universe!) Hubble used the telescope to study what was then referred to as the Andromeda Nebula.

Hubble could see the Andromeda Nebula contained many stars, like the Milky Way, but dimmer. Hubble calculated the distance of the Andromeda Nebula and based on his results, Hubble determined that Andromeda was not a cloud within the Milky Way, it was a distinct galaxy. The implications of this finding were huge.

Suddenly, the universe was much, much bigger than had been previously thought. It was a discovery on a similar scale to the Copernican Revolution, when science had moved from a geocentric model of the cosmos to a heliocentric model. Earth was not at the center of the universe. The sun was not at the center of the Milky Way. The Milky Way was not the only galaxy in the universe. Discovery by discovery, Earth played a progressively smaller role in the vast universe.

THE LAUNCH OF ASTROPHYSICS

Astrophysics and cosmology took off at the beginning of the twentieth century, marked by the exciting theories and discoveries made by Albert Einstein, Edwin Hubble, and their peers. Einstein and Hubble didn't just contribute new discoveries about the physics and dynamics of the universe, they also raised many new questions. Hubble's discovery of galaxies beyond our own necessitated further work to understand just what galaxies are and how they form, evolve, and interact. Einstein's theory of general relativity raised numerous questions about the effects of gravity on space-time, including what happened at the end of a star's life.

Matter accreting around a black hole has enough angular momentum that instead of falling straight in, it forms a disk and spirals inward.

The Modern Understanding of the Evolution of Stars and Galaxies

2

> *"The nitrogen in our DNA, the calcium in our teeth, the iron in our blood, the carbon in our apple pies were made in the interiors of collapsing stars. We are made of starstuff."*
> —Carl Sagan

M ost astronomers today believe that the universe began with a Big Bang about 13.8 billion years ago. At the moment of the Big Bang, the universe was infinitely dense and small and very hot before inflating rapidly. After inflation (one millionth of a second after the Big Bang), the expansion began to slow down. Protons and neutrons formed, and within a few minutes, those particles formed the nuclei of hydrogen, helium, and lithium. The universe continued to expand and cool until it became the vast, cold cosmos we know today.

After the Big Bang, the remnant heat from the Big Bang manifested as different wavelengths of radiation, including X-rays and ultraviolet rays. As the universe expanded, the wavelengths of the radiation stretched, and by 300,000 years after the Big Bang, the radiation was in the form of what's called **cosmic microwave background** (CMB) radiation. Astrophysicists study the CMB using special space probes, such as the WMAP. In doing so, they can observe the conditions of the early universe from which the first galaxies formed, and they can build theories of how those first galaxies came into being. Scientists also observe fully formed galaxies using the light emitted by stars within them to study galactic structure and dynamics over time.

The Formation of Galaxies

Our current understanding of cosmology states that the first galaxies formed as a result of the small density fluctuations in the CMB. These density fluctuations grew in scale as the universe expanded. The force of gravity in the denser regions created clumps of hydrogen, dark matter (which we'll cover shortly), and some helium. When the clumps had enough density and mass such that the force of gravity overcame the clump's internal gas pressure, a threshold known as the **Jeans instability**, the clump began to collapse into the first structures.

As the clumps collapsed and became protogalaxies (the precursors to full-fledged galaxies), the gas cooled and fragmented. Due to the effects of gravity, the gas formed into the core of the protogalaxy while dark matter, which interacts weakly with gravity, formed a halo around the core. The density within the protogalaxy increased, creating gas clouds within it, which collided and catalyzed star formation. If the star formation process was slow, the gas collisions created a rotating spiral disk, resulting in a spiral galaxy. If the star formation occurred in a single burst, the galaxy was a smooth, elliptical galaxy.

The first galaxies were much smaller than the galaxies we see today. Scientists believe that these dwarf galaxies have since merged together and formed larger galaxies. Galaxies tend to occur in proximity to other galaxies, either in groups of two or in galaxy clusters. Some galaxies have smaller orbiting satellite galaxies that tend to be redder and have less ongoing star formation than their central galaxy.

Galaxy Characteristics

There are two major types of galaxies: elliptical and spiral.

Elliptical galaxies have a bulge-like central region surrounded by a halo of old stars and old star clusters (globular clusters). They range from perfectly round to elliptical in shape and have no rotation. Because of the lack of

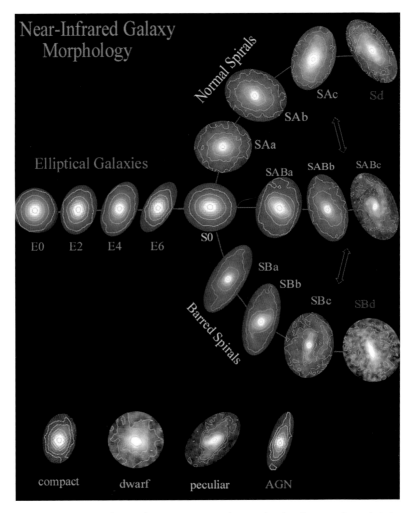

Near-Infrared Galaxy Morphology

Normal Spirals

SAc   Sd

SAb

SAa

Elliptical Galaxies

SABa   SABb   SABc

E0   E2   E4   E6

S0

SBa

SBb

Barred Spirals

SBc   SBd

compact   dwarf   peculiar   AGN

Lowercase letters indicate the compactness of a spiral galaxy's arms, from tightly wound (a) to loosely wound (c).

rotation, the orbits of stars within them is random, much like a swarm of bees. Elliptical galaxies tend to have little gas and dust (the birthplace of stars) and therefore tend to consist of older stars with little ongoing star formation. They range in size from dwarfs of just 0.3 kiloparsecs in diameter to (rare) giants that are hundreds of kiloparsecs in diameter. (A **parsec** is a distance of 3.26 light years, a kiloparsec is 3,262 light years.) Elliptical galaxies tend to occur in galaxy clusters.

Spiral galaxies such as the Milky Way are rotating galaxies with a center bulge surrounded by a flattened disk with spiral arms. It's likely that the center bulge formed in a single burst of star formation while the spiral arms formed later. Like elliptical galaxies, spiral galaxies also have a halo with globular clusters located around the disk. In contrast to elliptical galaxies, spiral galaxies tend to have a lot of gas and dust (primarily in the disk) and therefore have sites of ongoing star formation. Because the disk contains younger stars, it tends to be bluer than the older, redder central bulge. The typical diameter of a spiral galaxy's disk is between 5 and 100 kiloparsecs.

Spiral galaxies account for about 77 percent of galaxies in the universe. Some spiral galaxies have a bar in the center and are classified as barred spiral galaxies. Spiral galaxies are usually found in more isolated areas rather than galaxy clusters.

While scientists can easily study the different galaxy shapes, they are less certain about how different galaxy shapes came to be. Some believe that the spin of a collapsing gas cloud determined the type of galaxy it forms. The angular momentum of a spinning gas cloud would flatten the cloud and form the disk of a spiral galaxy, while a gas cloud without spin would have a rounder structure and become an elliptical galaxy. Others believe that elliptical galaxies are formed by

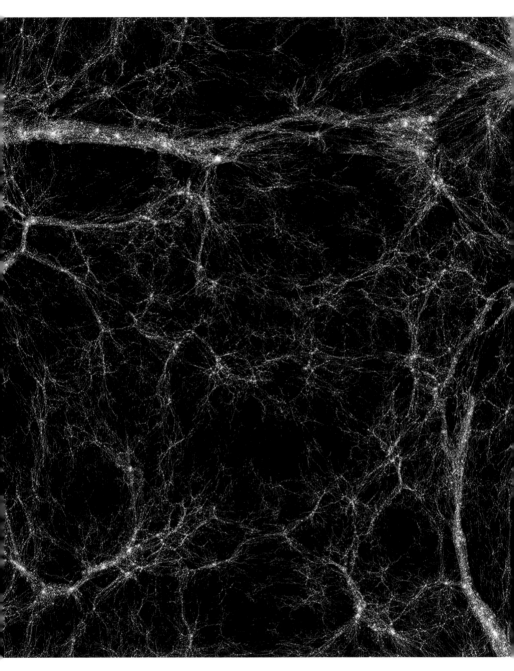

Filaments of dark matter may look delicate in pictures, but they can be larger than our own solar system.

the collision of spiral galaxies, which is why elliptical galaxies are common in galaxy clusters.

There are also irregular galaxies, which have shapes that do not fall into the other categories, and make up only two to three percent of all galaxies in the universe.

The Role of Dark Matter

In 1932, Dutch astronomer Jan Oort studied the motions of stars in the disk of the Milky Way galaxy and the gravitational influence of the galactic disk on these stars. He first calculated the velocity of the stars and was then able to calculate how much mass was required in the galactic disk to keep the stars in orbit in the galaxy rather than flying off into outer space. To his surprise, the required mass was three times the mass of the visible stars and nebulae in the Milky Way, which meant that there was "missing mass," or undetected matter.

Similarly, at Caltech in 1933, Swiss astronomer Fritz Zwicky studied the total light output of galaxies in the Coma Cluster, which gave a general idea of how much mass there was in the cluster. Zwicky calculated that there must be ten times more mass holding the galaxies in the Coma Cluster together than the mass accounted for by the light of the stars.

The missing mass is what astronomers now call dark matter, as the mass is present though not visible. Dark matter neither absorbs nor emits light and is visible only through its gravitational effects. If you took a snapshot of dark matter, however, it would reveal that between galaxies lies a cosmic web of sheets, filaments, and knots. Astrophysicists typically use "sheets, filaments, and knots" as visual descriptors to help us imagine what dark matter looks like through a comparison to everyday objects.

A snapshot of the gas in the universe would look very similar, with corresponding filaments of gas between galaxies and galaxies resting in the knots of the web. The distribution is similar because gas tends to follow dark matter due to its gravitational effects. It is thought that dark matter clumped first in the early universe due to the density fluctuations in the CMB and accelerated the aggregation of normal matter (gas in this case) into regions of higher density that collapsed into galaxies and then stars. It is therefore not surprising that astronomers have found that galaxies are situated in enormous haloes of dark matter.

In addition to inferring the presence of dark matter by calculating the mass required based on star velocity, astrophysicists can map dark matter through **gravitational lensing**, or the distortion and bending of light due to gravity. In 2012, astronomers used data from NASA's Chandra X-ray Observatory and other telescopes to map the distribution of dark matter in a galaxy cluster called Abell 383. By layering the X-ray image of the ordinary matter in the cluster with the gravitational lensing shown in the optical images, the team was able to make a map of the dark matter in Abell 383. They found that the distribution of dark matter in the cluster is shaped like a football.

The Expansive Forces of Dark Energy

In 1929, Hubble made another discovery that changed the way scientists understood the universe. At the time, many scientists including Einstein thought that the universe was unchanging in size. Einstein even added a cosmological constant Λ (the Greek letter lambda) to his general theory of relativity, representing an energy of empty space, to force his equations to predict a static state of the universe.

At Mount Wilson, with the Hooker telescope, Hubble studied forty-six different galaxies and found that the farther galaxies are apart from one another, the faster they move away from each other. He could measure this by looking at the galaxy's **redshift**, or the shifts in emission and absorption lines in an object's light spectrum. As an object in space moves away from us, its wavelengths stretch and become longer (redder). As a result, the unique emission and absorption lines of an object are shifted to longer wavelengths on the light spectrum. This effect is similar to the experience of changing sound we have when an ambulance goes by. The siren's sound waves are first compressed and then stretched as it approaches and then moves past us.

Discovering the
Accelerating Expansion

In 1998, two teams of astronomers raced to measure the expansion rate of the universe. They expected to find how fast the expansion was slowing, but they found a surprising result: it was actually speeding up. The findings shocked the scientific community, but both the Supernova Cosmology Project at the University of California at Berkeley and the High-Z Supernova Search Team independently arrived at the same result.

The teams studied Type 1a supernovas, which serve as standard candles (objects with a known, consistent, intrinsic brightness) to calculate the distance to far-off objects. By comparing the apparent brightness of a Type 1a supernova to its known intrinsic brightness, scientists can calculate the distance to that supernova.

The teams measured the distance to multiple supernovas, creating markers of the universe at several points in history. Then, they looked at the supernova's redshift to determine how much the universe had expanded since each of those points in time to plot the rate of expansion.

A supernova up close "would look blue, mostly, and that's a short wavelength of light. As the universe expands, everything that's in it that's not nailed down expands just with the universe, and that includes the very photons of light that are traveling to us from the distant supernova," said Saul Perlmutter, leader of the Supernova Cosmology Project in an interview with NPR's *Fresh Air*. "What used to look blue with a short wavelength, by the time it reaches us looks a lot redder with a longer wavelength. We can just read off how much the universe has stretched by how much this wavelength has stretched and how red the light has gotten."

The implications: the expansion of the universe has accelerated, not slowed, over billions of years.

Perlmutter and High-Z Supernova Search Team's leaders Brian Schmidt and Adam Reiss, shared a 2011 Nobel Prize for their work.

Hubble saw that the redshift increased as a linear function of distance, indicating that farther-away galaxies were moving away at a faster rate. Hubble concluded that the universe was expanding uniformly at a rate known as the Hubble Constant. The rate has been fine-tuned over time, and as of 2013, NASA estimated the Hubble Constant to be 70.4 kilometers per second for every megaparsec in distance. (A megaparsec is a distance of about 3.26 million light-years.)

When Hubble first showed the universe was expanding, scientists weren't sure how that expansion was changing and whether the universe would eventually contract into a Big Crunch. Whatever the answer, they thought, the expansion would inevitably slow due to the attractive force of gravity.

In 1998, however, images of very far off supernovas from the Hubble Space Telescope (named after Edwin Hubble) showed otherwise. Far-off galaxies are moving away from us faster than expected, signifying an accelerating expansion of the universe. There are increasing amounts of space between galaxies, and the universe is getting progressively less dense. The discovery marked a fundamental shift in how astronomers understand the dynamics and composition of the universe.

What's behind the accelerating expansion? We don't know, but scientists call it dark energy. Taking into account the rate of the universe's expansion as well as the contracting effects of gravity, astrophysicists can then calculate the density the universe must have to maintain its expansion rate. When scientists used WMAP (a NASA space probe that surveys the entire sky) data to add up the amount of ordinary matter and the amount of dark matter, the total accounted for only 32 percent (5 percent ordinary matter plus 27 percent dark matter) of the effective density needed to maintain the current expansion rate. Hence, about 68 percent of the universe is unaccounted for when we look at the matter present, and it is this missing density that we call dark energy.

THE EVOLUTION OF STARS

Stars are born in extremely cold clouds of gas and dust. The cold temperatures cause atoms to bind together within the molecular clouds and the gas to clump in regions of high density. A dense clump will break off from the molecular cloud and begin to spin due to angular momentum. Eventually, the clump begins to collapse inward due to the weight of gravity, and a star is underway.

Stellar Evolution

The lifecycle of a star varies based on its mass, but we can use the lifecycle of a star with the mass of the sun as a good model. Astronomers often use a diagram called the Hertzsprung-Russell (H-R) Diagram that plots the absolute magnitude (luminosity) of stars and their color, which

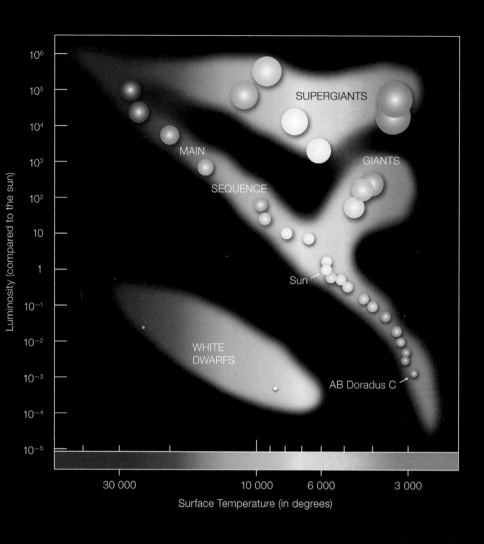

Brighter stars appear higher on the main sequence and also more massive, a correlation known as the Mass Luminosity relation.

correlates to temperature. The resulting diagram shows a strong correlation between the temperature and luminosity of a star, which is further correlated to its stage of stellar evolution. In the H-R diagram, stars in a steady state of burning hydrogen fall on the Main Sequence, which follows a band from the bottom right to the upper left of the diagram. When a star runs out of hydrogen in its core, it moves off the Main Sequence into other corners of the diagram.

The interstellar cloud breaks up into fragments due to gravitational instabilities, creating the seeds of multiple stars or clusters of stars. At this point, the clouds are huge (tens of light years across) and very cold (about 10 to 20 degrees **Kelvin**, or 10 to 20 degrees above absolute zero). As a clump contracts due to the gravitational effects of its own weight, atoms within the clump begin to collide more often and create heat from friction. The gas fragment starts to warm.

The central density of the gas fragment increases, and the size of the clump decreases to about 0.1 light years across. The gas cloud is now about 100 degrees Kelvin, and the increased heat agitates the atoms and creates faster velocities and more collisions. As the fragment becomes more compact and pressurized, fragmentation stops. This section of the original gas cloud is on its way to stardom.

As the fragment collapses, it becomes increasingly dense, hot, and pressurized. When the pressure becomes strong enough to resist additional infall (inward movement) of gas, the protostar stabilizes.

A few million years after the gas cloud began to contract, the protostar becomes a star. At this point, the central

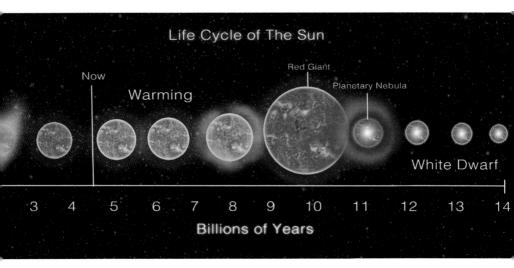

Life Cycle of The Sun

Now

Warming

Red Giant

Planetary Nebula

White Dwarf

3 4 5 6 7 8 9 10 11 12 13 14

Billions of Years

When a white dwarf cools entirely, it will transition into a black dwarf, but no black dwarfs have formed yet.

temperature reaches millions of degrees Kelvin (for a star with the mass of our sun), and thermonuclear fusion begins: hydrogen protons begin to fuse into helium protons in a process called the proton-proton cycle. (Stars more massive than the sun follow a different nuclear fusion process called the carbon-nitrogen-oxygen cycle.) Thermonuclear fusion creates a stellar wind, which prevents the infall of new mass to the young star.

The star continues to become denser and hotter and becomes a Main Sequence star (as plotted on the H-R diagram). Main Sequence stars burn hydrogen into helium, and the gas pressure generated in the core resists the force of gravity in a state of equilibrium. Main Sequence stars account for about 90 percent of the stars in the universe. The star will spend about 99 percent of its lifetime, typically billions of years, in this stage of its life.

Almost 10 billion years after it forms, the star begins to run of out hydrogen in the core. As nuclear fusion ceases, the pressure in the core drops and the star is no longer in equilibrium with gravity. Meanwhile, hydrogen continues to combust in the intermediate layers of the star. The core begins to contract due to the loss of pressure, density increases, and heat increases. The increased temperature causes the hydrogen in the star's intermediate layers to fuse faster while the newly increased gas pressure causes the outermost layers to expand to about 100 times their previous size. As the surface expands, it cools and becomes red (like metal cooling from white hot to glowing red). A star in this phase of stellar evolution is called a **red giant**, which is seen to the upper right of the H-R diagram.

The core of the red giant is incredibly dense, compressed, helium gas. As the density increases, the pressure builds again, and the helium begins to fuse into carbon. The core returns to equilibrium, and the hydrogen fusion in the outer layers slows down. The star shrinks, and the surface temperature increases. When the helium in the core becomes depleted, however, the carbon core shrinks and heats, and the hydrogen and helium fusion in the intermediate layers intensifies. Again, the outer layers expand from the new pressure, and the star again becomes a red giant.

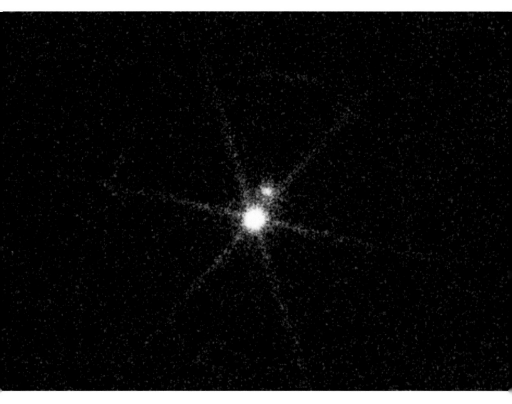

White dwarfs are often discovered through their effects on orbits of nearby stars, as seen with Sirius A and Sirius B.

For a star the size of the sun, the cycle of contracting, heating, fusing, and expanding stops here. For more massive stars, it continues, and heavier and heavier elements are formed. Once all fusion stops, the star collapses. Stars with masses similar to our sun eject most of their outer shell, creating a planetary nebula of glowing gas. (It's called a planetary nebula because when viewed with early telescopes, the far-off phenomena were dim and thought to be related to planets.) The remnant becomes a white dwarf, a very dense, small, cooling star plotted in the lower left corner of the H-R diagram. More massive stars die in supernova explosions, in which much of the stellar material blows off into space and leaves behind an incredibly dense core called a neutron star. The remnants of the most massive stars, however, turn into black holes.

Black Holes

The implications of Einstein's equations suggested that the biggest stars would collapse into a singularity: a point with no size but infinite density. These singularities are today known as black holes. When a star with about three times the mass of the sun dies, it explodes in a supernova, and the remnant collapses into a stellar black hole. A black hole is incredibly massive and compact and has gravity so strong that no matter or light can escape it. The boundary beyond which no light or information can escape is called the event horizon. As a black hole "eats" more mass, the event horizon increases in diameter.

Black holes were first predicted in the 1700s, but it took centuries before they were accepted by the scientific community. In the 1780s and 1790s, John Mitchell of Great Britain and Pierre-Simon de Laplace of France independently proposed the existence of bodies so massive, light cannot escape the attractive force of gravity. In 1916, German astronomer Karl Schwarzschild published the first full solutions to Einstein's general relativity equations and found a similar result. Still, few astrophysicists accepted the idea.

In the following decades, physicists continued to debate the end result of an imploding, massive star. In 1939, physicist J. Robert Oppenheimer and his graduate student Hartland Snyder published formulas detailing the implosion of a star into a black hole. American and Western European physicists remained skeptical, pointing out that Oppenheimer and Snyder relied on an idealized spherical star with no spin or radiation for their calculations.

World War II and the efforts to build an atomic bomb interrupted the theoretical research on black holes. Oppenheimer, for example, became the director of the Manhattan Project, which built the first atomic bombs. After the war, physicists including the theoretical physicist and Oppenheimer's fellow Manhattan Project veteran John Wheeler turned back to Oppenheimer and Snyder's predictions. As they again tackled the concept of black holes, this time they had powerful computational techniques and deeper knowledge of the laws of physics due to the experience they had gained building nuclear weapons.

In the early 1960s, physicists at the Livermore National Laboratory in California used computer simulations to show that the implosion of stars with a mass much greater than the sun produced black holes. These simulations, along with new frames of reference that made it easier to understand black holes, went a long way toward changing attitudes toward black holes. Significantly, John Wheeler turned from a black-hole skeptic to an evangelist for (and the person who named) black holes, helping turn them from an unpopular theory into a crucial component of modern astrophysics.

Astronomers cannot see black holes directly, but they can identify a black hole based on the distortion of space around it and its effect on nearby objects. Often, astronomers detect a stellar black hole by observing its effects on a nearby star. The outermost layers of the star are sucked into the black hole, and the matter emits x-ray radiation as it descends into the black hole.

Our current black-hole theory holds that there are also supermassive black holes and, possibly, miniature black holes. A supermassive black hole is between a million and a billion times more massive than a stellar black hole. Most galaxies have a supermassive black hole at the center, which we can detect by their effects on the orbits of nearby stars and gas. Astronomers don't yet know how supermassive black holes form. Some think that supermassive black holes form from collapsing clouds of gas during galaxy formation. Others think that stellar black holes might merge during galaxy collisions to form supermassive black holes.

The third type of black hole, miniature black holes, has not yet been observed. It is possible, however, that black holes with a mass much smaller than the sun formed shortly after the Big Bang.

NEW MYSTERIES TO SOLVE

The twentieth century brought an enormous amount of discovery in the realm of astronomy and astrophysics. The rapid improvement in telescopes and imaging equipment as well as the impact of World War II and thermonuclear research played a big role in advancing what we know about stars, galaxies, and how they evolve.

At the same time, each new understanding brings new questions and mysteries. How precisely do galaxies form? What is the impact of dark matter in their evolution and structure? What is behind the dark energy propelling them away from one another? We know more about stars because we are able to study them more closely, due to their proximity and ongoing formation, but there are still many questions about the final state of the most massive stars: black holes.

Hubble also served as the Chief of the
External Ballistics Branch at the Aberdeen
Proving Ground during World War II.

Scientists, Mathematicians, and Engineers

3

M yriad astronomers and astrophysicists have worked on solving the mysteries of stars and galaxies over the last few centuries. It is outside the scope of this book to cover every contributor, but a few names stand out. William Herschel was one of the first to look at the universe and seek an explanation for how clusters of stars form. Albert Einstein's groundbreaking work on theories of gravity created new questions about what happens to massive stars when they die. Henrietta Swan Leavitt made discoveries about variable stars that supported Edwin Hubble's cosmos-shattering discoveries, which showed that there are galaxies beyond our own and that the universe is expanding. Fritz Zwicky was an early visionary when it came to dark matter, gravitational lensing, supernovas, and neutron stars. But it takes more than the work of individuals to map our universe. Teams of scientists use the latest technology to better understand the cosmos. This chapter looks at both standout scientists and the technology we use.

SIR WILLIAM HERSCHEL AND COSMOLOGY

Sir William Herschel was born Friedrich Wilhelm Herschel in Hanover, Germany, in 1738. His father was a musician, and Herschel began his career in music as well. At 14, Herschel joined a local regiment band as an oboist. In 1757, the French invaded Hanover during the Seven Years' War, a prelude to the World Wars, and young Herschel fled to England. He started out copying music and eventually became a music teacher, performer, and composer. In 1766, Herschel became the organist of the Octagon chapel in Bath, England. As previously mentioned, in 1772, he brought his sister Caroline to Bath to serve as his assistant.

Herschel had a strong passion for astronomy, and after reading a book on optics, William and Caroline began grinding mirrors and building telescopes. He even melted the metal for his mirrors in the basement of his house. At first, Herschel focused on looking for double stars, and while making his observations, he discovered Uranus in 1781. After discovering Uranus, the Herschels became famous in astronomy. He received the Copley Medal from the Royal Society of London, which recognizes outstanding achievements in scientific research. (Other winners include Benjamin

Franklin, Albert Einstein, Charles Darwin, and Stephen Hawking.) He also received a pension and appointment as astronomer to King George III, which prompted Herschel and his sister Caroline to move close to Windsor Castle.

Herschel was knighted in 1816 and died in 1822.

ALBERT EINSTEIN AND THE PROPERTIES OF SPACE-TIME

Albert Einstein, one of the most influential physicists in history, was born in Ulm, Germany, on March 14, 1879 to a Jewish family. His family moved to Munich soon after his birth, where Einstein attended school until age 15. Contrary to popular mythology, Einstein was a top student, though he disliked the rote learning he experienced in his Munich school. Einstein left school in 1894 to join his family in Italy.

Einstein eventually finished high school in Switzerland at a school that he loved, and in 1900, he graduated with a degree from the Zurich Polytechnic Institute. He took a job at the Swiss patent office in Bern in 1902 and worked there for seven years, doing his assigned duties quickly and devoting the remaining time to physics. During that time, he married a former classmate, Mileva Marić, with whom he had one daughter (born before their marriage and given up for adoption) and two sons. (He and Marić later divorced, but Marić played a significant role in Einstein's work before that time.)

Einstein published several papers in the German Yearbook of Physics in 1905, including a paper on the photoelectric effect that earned Einstein a Nobel Prize in physics and a paper unveiling his special theory of relativity. Among other things, his special theory of relativity proposed that the speed of light is a constant, that mass and energy are two parts of the same thing (as shown in his famous equation $E=mc^2$), and that observers moving at different speeds witness time moving at different speeds. Another of the five papers, on the size of molecules, became the doctoral dissertation he submitted to the University of Zurich to earn a long-awaited PhD.

Following the success of his publications, Einstein took positions as a professor and researcher at universities in Zurich, Prague, and Berlin. In 1915, Einstein followed up his special theory of relativity with a general theory of relativity, which accounted for the laws of gravity, space, and time.

According to Einstein, gravity was not a force, it was a property of distorted space-time. Objects follow straight lines through space-time, but space-time itself is curved by mass. One of the ways he provided to prove his theory was through the observations of starlight during a solar eclipse. Due to the mass of the sun, light from the stars would bend, and the stars would appear to be in a different position than normal—and they would be visible due to the darkness from the eclipse. Just four years later, in 1919, a solar eclipse occurred as the sun crossed the Hyades star cluster, and the observations of starlight before and during the eclipse supported Einstein's work. Einstein's general theory of relativity and his global fame were established.

Einstein was in the United States when Hitler came to power in 1933, and he never returned to Germany. He became a faculty member at the Institute for Advanced Studies in Princeton, where he focused on general relativity, quantum theory, and a unified field theory. He lived a quiet life and enjoyed playing the violin, sailing, and taking walks in the country.

As tension grew worldwide, he became a strong advocate for peace and nuclear control. Despite his pacifism, Einstein's famous equation $E=mc^2$ was an essential part of developing the atomic bomb. In 1952, Einstein was asked to serve as the second president of Israel (a largely ceremonial figurehead position), but he declined. He did not think the position suited his personality or aptitudes.

Einstein died in 1955 from a brain aneurysm.

HENRIETTA SWAN LEAVITT AND THE LUMINOSITY OF VARIABLE STARS

Henrietta Swan Leavitt is famous for her work deciphering the relationship between period and **luminosity** in variable (pulsating) stars, which helped astronomers determine a variable star's distance. This work became very important

A Swedish mathematician sought to nominate Leavitt for a 1926 Nobel Prize, but Leavitt had died quietly a few years before.

when Hubble used the relationship to determine the distance of stars in what was then called the Andromeda Nebula, and again when Hubble calculated the distance of galaxies compared to their movement away from us.

Leavitt was born in Cambridge, Massachusetts, in 1868. She studied at Oberlin College for two years before moving to the Society for Collegiate Instruction of Women (today named Radcliffe College). She studied astronomy in her senior year of college and took another course in astronomy after she graduated from college in 1892. She suffered a serious illness that left her profoundly hearing-impaired, but her deafness didn't stop her from pursuing her love of astronomy. Leavitt became a volunteer assistant at Harvard Observatory in 1895 and joined the staff there in 1902.

Leavitt was assigned to work on a project to determine the brightness of all measurable stars. While doing so, Leavitt discovered a relationship between the length of a variable star's pulsations (period) and its luminosity. By knowing the true brightness of the star and comparing that measurement to its apparent brightness, astronomers could then calculate the distance to that star. (It's much like seeing an oncoming car at night and judging its distance based on the apparent brightness of the headlights.)

Leavitt published her work in 1912, and her methodology for measuring distances became a strategy for calculating the distances of galaxies far, far away. Modern technology allows for more accurate methods, but at the time, Leavitt's work was an essential tool for astronomers, including Hubble, who were making fundamental discoveries about the universe.

Leavitt became the head of the Harvard Observatory's photographic stellar photometry department, where she developed standards of photographic measurements. She died in 1921.

EDWIN HUBBLE AND THE UNIVERSE BEYOND THE MILKY WAY

Edwin Hubble was born in 1889 in Marshfield, Missouri, and moved to Wheaton, Illinois, soon after his birth.

Hubble studied mathematics and astronomy at the University of Chicago, graduating in 1910. He became one of the first Rhodes Scholars at Oxford, where he studied law as well as literature and Spanish. He returned home and became a high school teacher and basketball coach before beginning

The Air and Space Museum at the Smithsonian

The Air and Space Museum at the Smithsonian has a significant collection of objects that unveil the history of astronomy and study of the universe, including the telescopes William Herschel and Edwin Hubble used in their discoveries. The Air and Space Museum is the largest of the Smithsonian's nineteen museums and attracts more than eight million people each year. The Air and Space Museum is spread across two locations in Washington, DC, and Chantilly, Virginia.

The *Explore the Universe* exhibit in Washington, DC, examines the history and progression of astronomical instruments. The exhibit first shows how astronomers studied the universe with the naked eye and then presents how different fields from photography to spectroscopy changed what we can see and learn. The exhibit includes astrolabes used by Islamic astronomers, handheld instruments that helped solve astronomical problems and map the universe. The exhibit contains Herschel's 20-foot (6-meter) telescope, which was his favorite of the telescopes he built, as well as the observing cage from the 100-inch (254-centimeter) Hooker Telescope where Edwin Hubble would sit while studying nebulae and galaxies in the 1920s and 1930s. It also includes early **spectrographs** used to take photos of light spectrum to study redshift and a 8.2-foot (2.5-meter) backup mirror and the original camera from the Hubble Space Telescope.

For those who are not in the Washington, DC, area, there's an online version of the exhibition that presents the same historical progression from naked eye to current technology and research.

his doctoral degree in astronomy. Hubble was invited to join the staff of the Mount Wilson Observatory in California, but as soon as Hubble had finished his PhD thesis and defense, he enlisted in the army and sailed for France. When Hubble returned from serving in World War I in 1919, he went straight back to Mount Wilson Observatory and began his career as an astronomer.

Hubble was an ambitious astronomer and hoped to win the Nobel Prize for his paradigm-shifting discoveries about the universe beyond the Milky Way and its expansion. During his lifetime, however, the Nobel Prize in physics typically did not recognize accomplishments in astronomy. Hubble spent much of his later life working to include astronomy under the branch of physics, but the Nobel Prize Committee did not change their eligibility standards until shortly after Hubble's death.

According to a stamp released by the United States Postal Service in 2008 to honor Hubble, "Often called a 'pioneer of the distant stars,' astronomer Edwin Hubble (1889–1953) played a pivotal role in deciphering the vast and complex nature of the universe ... Had he not died suddenly in 1953, Hubble would have won that year's Nobel Prize in Physics."

FRITZ ZWICKY AND THE DUNKLE MATERIE

Fritz Zwicky was the first to point out the existence of dark matter, or *dunkle materie,* as he called it in a 1933 paper published in a German-Swiss journal. Zwicky was born in 1898 in Varna, Bulgaria, to a Swiss family. He was educated in Switzerland, where his father's family originated, before moving to Pasadena, California, in 1925 to work at Caltech. He started as an assistant and eventually became Caltech's first professor of astrophysics. It was an exciting time to be in Pasadena, which is near the Mount Wilson Observatory where Edwin Hubble was studying the universe with the Hooker Telescope.

Zwicky studied galaxies and theorized that if a star could bend the light of a more distant object, as Einstein predicted, a galaxy would bend that light even more. He argued that galaxies gathered in clusters, contrary to the popular belief at the time that galaxies were evenly distributed. Using the Coma Cluster of galaxies, he wrote that there must be dark matter to account for the rate of galaxies within the cluster.

Zwicky was also one of the first to hypothesize that some stars explode in very bright bursts that he and Mount Wilson astronomer Walter Baade called supernovas. Supernovas, they suggested, produced cosmic rays and very small, ultra-dense stars made of tightly packed neutrons. Their hypotheses were later proven to be correct. Zwicky accurately predicted the existence of a neutron star inside the Crab Nebula, which was the debris from a supernova explosion. Using a new telescope on Palomar Mountain, Zwicky discovered 122 supernovas in total, more than half of the supernovas known to exist at the time of his death.

Zwicky also worked on rocketry and propulsion systems during and post-World War II, for which he won the United States Medal of Freedom in 1949. Zwicky was an inventive worker and was awarded more than fifty patents, many related to rockets.

Zwicky is often remembered for insulting his colleagues, and it is thought that this limited the formal awards and historical acknowledgement he garnered for his work. Nevertheless, it is true that Zwicky was a pioneer in many areas of astronomy and astrophysics, especially around dark matter.

THE TECHNOLOGY USED TO STUDY DISTANT STARS AND GALAXIES

Over and over in astronomy, major discoveries come from certain telescopes, instruments, and observatories. The Hubble Space Telescope. The Keck Observatory. UMAP and the SDSS. Many of the different instruments capture very different images of the sky, helping scientists put together a bigger picture of stars and galaxies and the forces that shape them.

The major difference between most telescopes and instruments is the portion of the electromagnetic spectrum they capture. Some take images of visible light, others study objects in the infrared, while others look at microwave, X-ray, or UV radiation. Different types of cosmic phenomena at different distances from Earth (and times in history) emit varying wavelengths of light, and having the ability to study space at different parts of the electromagnetic spectrum is essential. Other differentiating factors include the size of the mirrors and what aspect is most important to get in high quality, such as precision or scope of image.

Studying the CMB to Uncover the Evolution of the Universe

Over the last few decades, scientists have sent three different space probes on discovery missions to map the CMB radiation left over from the Big Bang. (A probe is a spacecraft without any humans on board that travels through space to collect data to send back to Earth.) Since the Big Bang, CMB radiation has been stretched out and cooled by the expansion of the universe. All three probes used differential microwave radiometers, instruments that study radiation and measure the temperature differences between two points. The devices separate the light from sources in our own galaxy and other galaxies, which are closer to us in space and time than the CMB radiation. The CMB measurements they produce give astronomers important clues as to the evolution of the universe and formation of the first galaxies and stars.

The temperature differences WMAP mapped (and which grew into galaxies) were less than one-millionth of a degree.

NASA launched COBE, the Cosmic Background Explorer, in 1989 as the first space probe sent to make a full map of the CMB. The first results came back in 1992 and while limited in resolution, they showed that the CMB is nearly completely homogenous excepting small fluctuations in temperature.

In 2001, NASA launched another probe to improve on the data from COBE, the Wilkinson Microwave Anistropy Probe (WMAP). Over nine years of flight, WMAP's data produced the first detailed, full-sky map of the CMB radiation. Studying the WMAP data produced a more precise estimate of the age of the universe, 13.75 billion years. It showed us the appearance of the first stars (about 400 million years post-Big Bang) and the small fluctuations in density that seeded the first galaxies. The data estimated the composition of the universe as 4.6 percent ordinary (**baryonic**) matter, 23 percent dark matter, and 72 percent dark energy. WMAP also showed that the universe is most likely flat.

Altogether, WMAP produced results that changed astronomers' ability to understand the universe with precision. WMAP's results were some of the most cited results in scientific papers worldwide in 2011 and 2012, among other years, and the WMAP team won the 2012 Gruber Prize for its impact on cosmology.

After WMAP's mission, the European Space Agency launched the Planck satellite to make CMB measurements with even greater precision and angular resolution. For example, Planck refined the proportions of matter at 4.9 percent ordinary matter, 26.8 percent dark matter, and 68.3 percent dark energy. Compared to the WMAP data, this estimate shows more dark matter and less dark energy. Planck's data also showed that the universe was 13.8 billion years old, slightly older than the estimate from the WMAP data.

Ground Telescopes

When telescopes were first invented, they were relatively small instruments held up toward the stars, like the telescopes of Galileo and Newton. Over time, these telescopes grew significantly in size and complexity and today are often housed in large observatories.

One major Keck discovery is the supermassive black hole at the center of the Milky Way, discovered by astronomer Andrea Ghez.

The W.M. Keck Observatory is located on top of the 13,796-foot (4,205 m) Mauna Kea volcano in Hawaii. The observatory contains two enormous telescopes that stand eight stories tall and weigh 300 tons. The mirrors are composed of thirty-six hexagonal components and are each 33 feet (10 meters) in diameter. The telescopes are the world's largest optical and infrared telescopes.

The area around the observatory is very calm, as the ocean around Hawaii is quiet, and there is little light pollution and few interfering weather conditions. NASA, Caltech, and the University of California are partners in Keck, and all have dedicated Keck time to use for research and discovery, as does the University of Hawaii, which provides access to Mauna Kea.

The Keck telescopes produce very clear images of outer space, down to nanometer precision, partly because of a new technique called adaptive optics. Adaptive optics measure and correct for atmospheric turbulence, which produces images that are ten times more clear than previous ground-based telescopes (including Keck before the adaptive optics were installed).

Keck's two telescopes can also work as an interferometer, two telescopes working together to act as if they were one large telescope. With this functionality, Keck has been instrumental in studying the areas around central black holes in galaxies that would otherwise require a telescope with a diameter of 100 meters or more. In total, scientists publish about 150 papers per Keck telescope per year, which is a greater scientific output than any other ground-based observatory in the world.

The Sloan Digital Sky Survey (SDSS) is a survey that has been mapping the universe since 1998 from the Apache Point Observatory in New Mexico. Fifty-one member institutions and over one thousand scientists from around the world collaborated in the latest data collection phase (called SDSS-III), which was released in 2014.

The SDSS began with a 2.5-meter optical telescope and now also includes a second telescope in Chile that provides observations from the Southern Hemisphere. The SDSS has various spectrographs that gather data by splitting the light from an observed object into its component wavelengths like a prism separates light into the colors of the rainbow.

SDSS-III, the latest phase of released data, focused on measuring light spectra from individual stars and galaxies using a fiber-optic spectrograph. The light intensities at different wavelengths tell astronomers about which kinds of atoms and molecules they're observing, which gives important information about both the movement of stars and galaxies as well as their chemical composition. The light spectra and breakdown of elements also helps scientists study the evolution of those stars and galaxies, providing insight into the history of the universe. Other components of the SDSS-III data phase include near-infrared examination of stars throughout the Milky Way (looking at stars in near-infrared wavelengths helps see through dust clouds).

SDSS astronomers also used spectrographs to study baryon acoustic oscillations (BAOs) and quantify the expansion of the universe, dark matter, and dark energy. In the first million years after the Big Bang, sound waves bounced through the ionized gas, excited by the interaction of gravity and pressure in areas of greater density. The imprints of the sound waves are observable today and provide a second way to measure the expansion of the universe (in addition to the supernova technique that uses redshifted Type 1a supernovas to measure how fast distant objects are receding from us).

Space Telescopes

For many years, scientists were limited primarily to data gathered from telescopes on Earth. Telescopes grew increasingly powerful between the 1600s and the twenty-first century, but scientists were still hampered by distortion caused by Earth's atmosphere and the interference from clouds and light pollution. In 1990, NASA launched the Hubble Space Telescope, the first major optical telescope in space. It orbits Earth at about 17,000 miles per hour, taking pictures of planets, stars, and galaxies from its unique vantage point.

Hubble is very accurate. It can aim its telescope at specific points in space with the same precision as someone shining a laser beam on a dime located 200 miles away. With no interference from Earth's atmosphere, Hubble can also see tiny objects in space, producing images that are the equivalent of seeing fireflies in Tokyo while sitting in Maryland. With this accuracy and incredible resolution, Hubble has been able to study very distant galaxies that show us the universe as it was billions of years ago.

In one particularly notable use of the Hubble Space Telescope, astronomers trained Hubble on an unremarkable

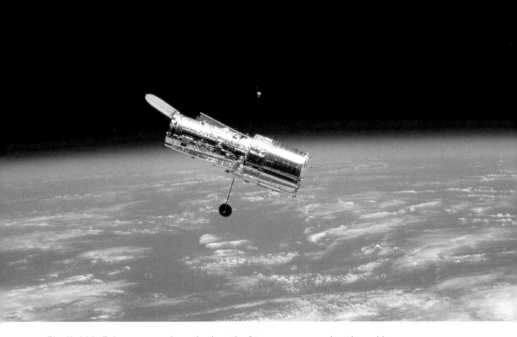

The Hubble Telescope was launched on the Discovery space shuttle and has traveled over three billion miles around Earth.

section of the sky. Hubble focused on this angle for ten days. (Usually astronomers would use Hubble for a very specific purpose for a matter of hours.) The resulting long-exposure image, called the Hubble Deep Field, showed 3,000 galaxies of varying sizes and shapes. In the far-off depths of the image, astronomers saw early, shapeless protogalaxies. Closer to us in space and time, astronomers could see galaxies colliding, merging, and growing. In the regions closest to us, Hubble showed fully-formed galaxies like our own. It was the first clear look back into the ancient universe and provided a sort of fossil record connecting the early universe to today.

Hubble images have also shown the impact of galaxy mergers. For example, Hubble was the first telescope to show individual stars in the Andromeda galaxy. The stars in the halo of the galaxy were much younger than expected, which suggests that they arrived in Andromeda via collisions between Andromeda and younger galaxies.

On a stellar level, Hubble has provided images of the planetary nebula (beautiful formations made from layers of gas) that stars like our sun eject when they die. Hubble has shown images of supernovas, providing more insight into the death of larger stars and the formation of neutron stars and black holes. Specifically, Hubble has made observations of Supernova 1987A over two decades, showing how a supernova unfolds, as well as making ongoing observations of a supermassive star approaching supernova state. NASA expects to keep Hubble in use until at least 2018.

The Herschel Space Observatory, named after amateur astronomer William Herschel, contains an infrared telescope flown into space. In addition to a primary mirror 3.5 meters in diameter, Herschel includes two cameras and imaging spectrometers and a very high-resolution spectrometer. The European Space Agency launched Herschel in 2009 to study radiation from the far-infrared to the sub-millimeter wavelengths. At these wavelengths, Herschel can observe gas and dust that is too cold to emit light in the visible spectrum or even as X-rays. As a result, astronomers have used Herschel's data to observe the **interstellar medium**, molecular clouds, and the birth of stars and planets.

Herschel has worked in conjunction with the Planck space observatory to provide more detail about the early universe. Herschel's data showed that the early universe contained dense concentrations of galaxies that converted gas and dust into stars at a rate a few hundred to 1500 times faster than the Milky Way produces stars today.

Gaia, a spacecraft launched by the European Space Agency in December 2013, is currently on a mission to create a three-dimensional map of the Milky Way, charting the position and velocity of one billion stars (1 percent of all stars) within the galaxy. The motion of each star as it orbits the galactic center is largely determined by the motion of the star at its birth, which means that the data Gaia sends back will allow scientists to study the formation of the Milky Way galaxy. Gaia will likely also be valuable in helping scientists discover planets around other stars, far-off supernovas and quasars, and more.

Gaia orbits the sun at the second Lagrange (L2) point (a point 1.5 million km further from the sun than Earth, named after its discoverer Joseph Louis Lagrange). This point is advantageous because it allows spacecraft to make continuous observations without eclipses from the sun. (Other spacecraft including Herschel and Planck also orbit at the L2 vantage point.)

The Planck space telescope has made about a trillion observations, a volume of data that only a supercomputer can tackle.

Visualizing the Evolution of Stars and Galaxies

U nlike other scientists, astrophysicists do not have a lab where they can test the formation of a galaxy or the effects of supernova on subsequent star formation. Without a physical lab, astrophysicists turn to computer programs and simulations to model the universe and test hypotheses for how structures such as stars and galaxies form and evolve.

Simulations that study the formation and evolution of stars and galaxies typically run on supercomputers. To model such massive cosmological processes, scientists need the enormous processing power and speed supercomputers have to offer. They also rely heavily on parallel programming, a type of computing that takes a big problem and breaks it down into many smaller problems solved simultaneously. Without supercomputers and parallel programming, the number-crunching required to build a simulation could take thousands of years on ordinary desktop computers. The calculations still often take a long time to run, several months in some cases, but parallel programming's power is a drastic improvement over a personal computer.

PROGRAMMING THE UNIVERSE

There are two main types of programming that go into building a computer simulation. The first entails developing the simulation codes. The scientists dedicated to this task must take the physical models and equations that represent our best knowledge for how the universe works and put them into a computer program. Typically, this type of programming is done in the programming languages C or Fortran, which are well suited for supercomputers and scientific computing.

Once the program is built, the team will run their simulation. Supercomputers are very expensive, ranging from tens of millions of dollars up to $1 billion, so typically, a team will apply for time on a national supercomputer, such as the Pleiades supercomputer at NASA. (Time on the computers is granted based on merit, so teams must show that they're solving a significant or interesting problem with their simulation and that they are qualified and prepared to run the simulation.) When the run has finished, the program has produced terabytes of data in the form of number-filled computer files.

At this point, the second type of programming comes into play. With so many numbers, it's difficult to look at the files and make sense of the data. Thankfully, computer programming makes data analysis significantly easier. (In the tech industry, modeling and analyzing huge amounts of data is often called Big Data.) Using Python or other modern programming languages, the scientists can load and manipulate the data and turn it into visual models and movies that are easier to study.

With the power of supercomputers and data visualizations, scientists have made beautiful two- and three-dimensional simulations of the evolution of the universe, the structure of stars, galaxies, and intergalactic space, and the distribution of unseen mass and energy. Some are static; others are animated. The models don't just provide new ways to see the structure of the universe, they can also give scientists better intuition about the structure and motion of the cosmos. Models designed for scientific research can be more utilitarian at times, while models designed for outreach efforts tend to be more beautifully composed to convey the awe of the phenomena they represent.

An Early Simulation

The Lawrence Livermore Laboratory was created in 1952 in the middle of the Cold War in order to advance thermonuclear weapon development. The founders of

Livermore knew they'd need to incorporate computers to solve the enormous, complex problems of physics and mathematics in thermonuclear weapon design. In 1953, the lab received a UNIVAC-1, the first commercially available computer.

The lab played an important role in the early science of black holes when code used to design bombs was repurposed to simulate the implosion of a massive star. Staff physicist Stirling Colgate, who specialized in fluids and radiation, typically focused on weapons development and nuclear physics, but he had an interest in astrophysics as well.

Working with Edward Teller, a theoretical physicist known as the "father of the hydrogen bomb," Richard White, and Michael May, Colgate simulated stellar implosion, taking into account factors such as pressure, nuclear reactions, heat, mass ejection, and more. It took a few years to get the simulation right, but in the early 1960s it was good enough to provide concrete proof that when a star with a mass greater than two suns implodes, it produces a black hole. The simulation looked much like the process described by J. Robert Oppenheimer and Snyder in their 1939 paper. Soviet physicists in Moscow had produced similar simulations of stellar implosion into black holes.

The Millennium Simulation

In 2005, an international group of scientists called the Virgo Consortium traced the evolution of ten billion particles in

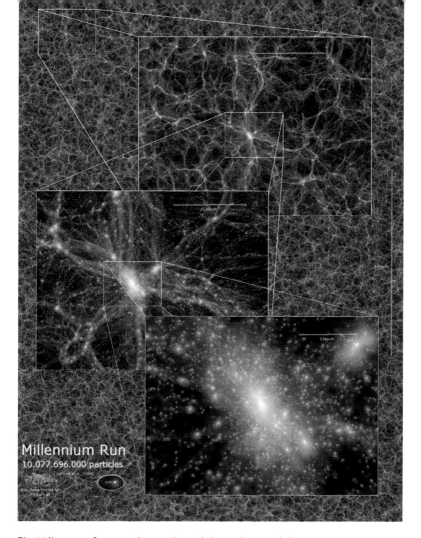

The Millennium Run simulation showed the evolution of about twenty million galaxies.

a cube of the universe that measured over two billion light years on each side. The Millennium Run, as it is called, ran for over a month on the primary supercomputer at the Max Planck Society's Supercomputing Centre in Germany. In the end, the astrophysicists had 25 terabytes of data, which they turned into a short three-dimensional movie showing a journey through the universe.

The Millennium Run included only the effects of gravity in its simulation, a force that is relatively simple to account for in a simulation.

The movie starts at the time when the universe was dominated by CMB radiation and progresses through the evolution of matter distribution. It shows filaments of dark matter (depicted in glowing neon colors) filled with bright galaxies interweaving around dark voids in space.

For the general population, the simulation is an interesting view of the structure of dark matter and galaxies in the universe. For astrophysicists, the simulation provided an opportunity to study the physics of galaxy and black hole formation. In particular, it helped reconcile the observations of supermassive black holes the SDSS found in the young universe with the gradual growth of structure predicted by the standard cosmological model.

More than 650 papers have been published using the data from the Millennium Run, which makes it one of the most significant astrophysical simulations in history.

The Eris Simulation

In 2011, a team of astrophysicists built a simulation that helped scientists understand how spiral galaxies like the Milky Way formed in a Lambda cold dark matter (LCDM) universe, the current standard cosmological paradigm (Lambda is a cosmological constant that accounts for dark

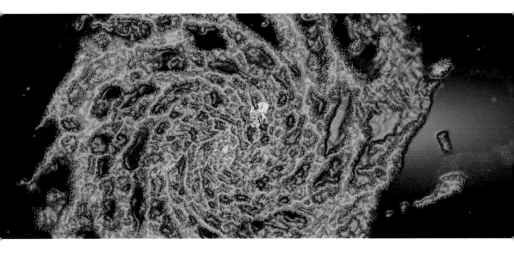

The Eris team allowed stars to form only at the highest density peaks in the simulation.

energy). Previous simulations had failed to produce realistic spiral galaxies. Specifically, many simulations couldn't capture both the observed structure of a galaxy as well as its matter content, and the resulting simulation ended up with overly large central bulges.

A team of researchers ran the Eris simulation on NASA's Pleiades supercomputer, with additional simulations run at the Swiss National Computing Center and the University of California Santa Cruz. The team built a very high-resolution simulation that included more than sixty million particles of dark matter and gas, plus the physics of gravity, hydrodynamics, and many other cosmological processes.

First, they built a low-resolution simulation of dark matter forming the kind of halos that surround present-day galaxies. Then, they "rewound" the simulation to find early conditions before drilling in and adding particles to create a higher resolution simulation. The high resolution was important because it allowed for more realistic distributions of matter and therefore more realistic distributions of stars in the resulting galaxy.

The simulation also included the impact of strong, localized supernovas. Supernovas play an important role in the formation of a spiral galaxy because they expel gas from the central bulge (where it would otherwise form stars and create a large bulge) and into the disks. At the end of the simulation, they had a spiral galaxy with a small bulge and large disk, similar to the Milky Way.

KIPAC Simulations

The Kavli Institute for Particle Astrophysics and Cosmology (KIPAC) at Stanford University creates many cosmological simulations designed to uncover galaxy formation, growth, and mergers. One of the questions KIPAC is trying to answer is why our galaxy, the Milky Way, doesn't have any satellite galaxies orbiting it. Simulations suggest that it should have such orbiting galaxies, but we haven't observed any. Is our galaxy unique, or are we missing the galaxies when we look for them? KIPAC is also trying to determine how galaxies are affected by their surroundings, and how their surroundings are affected by the galaxies themselves.

The Hayden Planetarium's Space Theater provides a realistic view of planets, star clusters, nebulae, and galaxies.

Some of these simulations are turned into videos shown at planetariums and IMAX theaters across the country, including the Hayden Planetarium in New York City. The videos have been narrated by popular actors including Whoopi Goldberg and Liam Neeson, with a goal of sharing astronomy with the general public.

Finding Hope in Simulations of the Vast Universe

Today, the Hayden Planetarium is a modern, spherical theater that appears to float in a 95-foot (29-meter) glass cube and shows simulations such as those created by KIPAC. The original Hayden Planetarium, however, was built in 1935 in the midst of the Great Depression. It was two stories high with a copper-covered, Art Deco-style dome and only the fourth planetarium to be built in the United States. It was funded in large part by a loan from the Reconstruction Finance Corporation, a government agency that financed entities from railroads and financial institutions to agriculture and local public works.

The main attraction was an auditorium in the dome that showed the night sky as it appeared today, thousands of years in the past, and thousands of years in the future. A huge projector called the Zeiss projector cast 4,500 stars on the dome by shining light through copper foil punched with tiny holes of varying sizes. For many New Yorkers accustomed to skies washed out by light pollution, seeing so many stars was a breathtaking event.

Over the next decade, new equipment allowed the planetarium to show auroras, solar eclipses, and more. The shows were theatrical events intended to share scientific research and boost public morale. The people behind the Hayden Planetarium hoped that showing the size and scale of the universe would help reduce public anxiety about the Great Depression.

Charles Hayden, a banker who helped fund the planetarium (and its namesake), said in the *New York Times*, "I think anything is beneficial that makes man realize there exists a much greater power in the universe than the human being on earth, and I feel that what one sees and hears in the Planetarium should make him stop, look and listen and realize this fact."

A desire for a more modern facility to share cutting-edge science and astrophysics led to the current planetarium, which opened in 2000.

The Illustris Project

In 2014, a team of astrophysicists released a new simulation called Illustris. The Illustris simulation is unique because it shows an enormous portion of the universe—it created a cube 350,000 light years across—at a high resolution that allows for detailed observation. It is also notable for its ability to simulate gas processes, which is much harder than simulating the effects of gravity. The properties of gas are important to

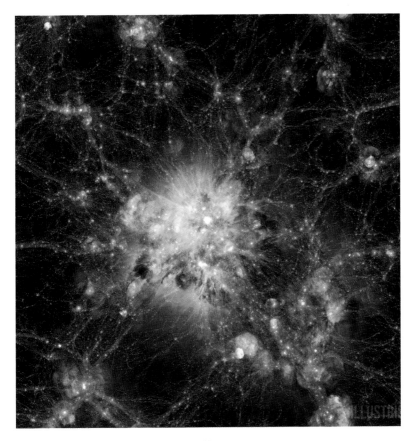

A simulation of gas processes from the Illustris project

account for, however, because galaxies form out of gas, and stars form from gas within those galaxies.

Illustris begins twelve million years after the Big Bang, just as dark matter is beginning to clump together. Ordinary matter follows suit and, over time, galactic clusters form in the cosmic web. The resulting simulated universe is very similar to the observed universe, which indicates again that our standard cosmological model is accurate.

Interstellar Simulation

In 2014, the science fiction film *Interstellar* introduced audiences to the effects of a black hole. The film relied on the time dilation that Einstein's physics predict, namely that time passes at different rates for people moving at different speeds. To create the effect they wanted, they'd need to create its cause: a massive black hole. Retired Caltech astrophysicist Kip Thorne advised on the science behind the movie to ensure that the simulation was accurate, black hole and all.

Like in academic simulations, Thorne started by plugging in the equations of physics that guide our universe. He then rendered the effects of the black hole's gravity on light. The resulting simulation of the black hole was not just accurate, it helped Thorne make a new discovery: the gravity of the black hole warped the light from the accretion disk they built around it. The accretion disk didn't appear much like a disk at all, but due to gravitational lensing, it appeared both above and below the black hole as well as in front of it. Much more research will come out on the topic, but Thorne and other scientists were very excited by the image the data produced.

THE PAST AND THE PRESENT

Simulations often focus extensively on past times. How did galaxies form? How did the stars in the Milky Way evolve? They help astrophysicists learn so much more about the ancient history of our universe. At the same time, they have an enormous effect on the future of astrophysics. When a simulation shows something new to astrophysicists, or when a simulation fails to perfectly recreate some aspect of the cosmos, it provides new directions of study.

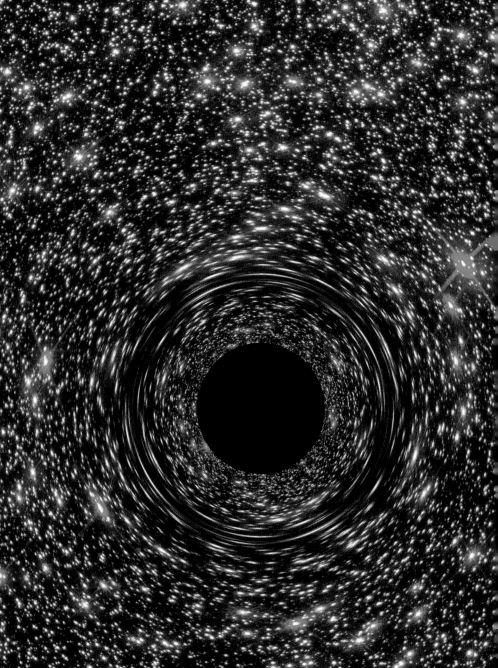

Supermassive black holes spin extremely fast, some at nearly the fastest rate allowed by general relativity.

The Evolution
of Stars and
Galaxies Today
and Tomorrow

5

S ome of the biggest questions in astronomy today involve the very things we cannot see: black holes, dark matter, and dark energy. Studying these elements of the universe and their effect on the evolution of stars and galaxies requires innovative thinking and powerful technology.

THE FUTURE

We cannot see inside of black holes, thus our information about them is limited to what we can infer by their effect on their surroundings. To some degree, the interest in black holes may be driven by the fact that they are so mysterious. We want what we cannot have, and in this case, it's certainty. However, knowing more about black holes can also tell us more about their effects on galactic and stellar evolution.

While there are many areas of ongoing research around black holes, here we will review two of the big topics.

According to British theoretical physicist Stephen Hawking, astrophysicists solved most of the major problems about black hole theory before they had any observational evidence of black holes. Classic theoretical physics states that any light or information that goes into a black hole will never return. Hawking dove into **quantum theory** (a theory of matter and energy based on the laws that govern the tiniest particles) and predicted that black holes do emit energy in the form of photons and other tiny particles, called Hawking radiation. Tiny bit by tiny bit, black holes will lose energy, and if they do not gain new mass, eventually disappear. Hawking's theory has not yet been proven and remains a topic of ongoing research.

One of the related questions explored in this research is, if radiation is emitted, can information be recovered? According to Hawking, any information that might be emitted would be like the smoke and ashes of a burnt encyclopedia — it would exist, but not in a useful form.

Another area of black hole research focuses on supermassive black holes. In April of 2016, a team of scientists published a report of a black hole 17 billion times the size of the sun in the peer-reviewed journal *Nature*. The largest black hole ever recorded at this time is 21 billion solar masses, but its measurement is much less certain.

Whether or not the new black hole discovery is the largest or simply one of the largest black holes ever recorded, it was notable that it was discovered in a cluster of average-sized galaxies. It's the first time scientists have found such a massive black hole in such an ordinary location, and it suggests that supermassive black holes are more common than previously thought. It also provides insight into what happens when black holes merge and the effect on galaxies.

In this case, the scientists believe that two galaxies merged (a common occurrence) and the black holes merged to create the supermassive black hole seen today, ejecting an enormous number of stars from the center of the galaxy.

GAMMA RAYS AND QUASARS

About once a day, satellites detect a huge amount of energy in the form of gamma-ray bursts. Gamma-ray bursts are incredibly bright—they are the brightest events known to occur in the universe—but most are billions of light years away and are a subject of ongoing research. The initial burst of gamma-ray radiation is followed by light emitted at longer wavelengths, such as x-ray and optical light. These afterglows provide material for scientists to study with optical spectroscopy, providing more information about how far away and how energetic the bursts are.

Scientists think that these gamma-ray bursts are the result of supernovas and signal the birth of a black hole. When a supermassive star collapses abruptly to become a black hole, they think, some of the gas is ejected to form an expanding shell of gas. Some of that gas falls into the black hole before being ejected again at a much faster rate. The jet collides with the expanding gas shell and explodes in a gamma-ray burst. These types of gamma-ray bursts can happen in less than a second or can last for hours.

Long gamma-ray bursts (twenty seconds or longer) are more common in galaxies with low metal contents, unlike our own.

Scientists are also researching the relationship between gamma rays and black holes in the production of quasars. Quasars (which stands for quasi-stellar radio sources) are incredibly bright objects that shine brighter than 100 normal galaxies combined. Despite this brightness, the region of intense light is usually significantly smaller than a single galaxy. The current theory is that quasars are the center of active galaxies, and the light is the result of gas spiraling into the supermassive black hole at the center.

As gas spirals inward under the gravitational attraction of the black hole, it accumulates in an accretion disk. Due to magnetic fields, some of the gas ends up channeled outward into jets of **plasma**, an ionized gas with essentially no electric charge that occurs in conditions with low pressure or very high temperatures. The plasma accelerates away from the center of the black hole at very nearly the speed of light (how the plasma does this is an area of continued research). The high-energy particles in the jet produce gamma ray light that can stretch large distances through space. Quasars can remain active for billions of years.

GALAXY FORMATION

The current LCDM cosmological model tells us that galaxies formed from fluctuations in density that caused molecular gas clouds to clump and condense into galaxies. Within that model, however, astrophysicists are still working to create a full understanding of how galaxies form. Major questions include:

- How did the first galaxies form?

- What determined the shapes and sizes of galaxies we see today?

Nuclear Bombs or Space Explosions?

Gamma-ray bursts, explosions with the power of 10 billion suns, were first discovered by United States military surveillance satellites in the 1960s. It was the midst of the Cold War, just a few decades after the United States dropped atomic bombs on Hiroshima and Nagasaki to end World War II with devastating effects, and fear of escalating nuclear warfare was high. In October of 1963, the United States, Great Britain, and the Soviet Union signed a Limited Test Ban Treaty that prohibited testing nuclear weapons in outer space, underwater, or in the atmosphere.

The United States feared that the Soviet Union might test nuclear weapons in space anyway, which the United States had no ability to monitor at the time. The same month as the treaty was signed, the United States Air Force launched a series of satellites called Vela satellites to monitor gamma rays, the longest-lasting radiation from an atomic bomb. The satellites were placed such that every part of Earth was under direct observation.

In 1965, scientist Ray Klebesadel of Los Alamos Scientific Laboratory took charge of the gamma ray instruments and began keeping records of events that triggered the detectors but were not nuclear explosions. In 1972, Klebesadel and two colleagues, Ian Strong and Roy Olsen, reviewed the data and found sixteen gamma-ray bursts of cosmic origin between 1969 and 1972. The earliest observed cosmic gamma-ray burst was in 1967. They published their findings in a paper that generated great excitement in the scientific community.

At the time, the source of the rays was a mystery, and many hypotheses centered on neutron stars. Neutron stars are very dense and have strong gravitational effects, but they aren't big enough to make a gamma-ray burst. Today, scientists think black holes are behind the bursts.

- How do central black holes affect the galaxies they inhabit?

- What causes star formation in a galaxy? Is it related to galaxy mergers, or does it happen within galaxies?

In one recent study, galaxy data analysis forced scientists to question their understanding of galaxy shapes and sizes. Most of the known giant galaxies are elliptical galaxies, and it was thought that this was always the case. In 2015, a team at the California Institute of Technology discovered giant "super spiral" galaxies by analyzing galaxies catalogued in the NASA Extragalactic Database. Three percent of the most luminous galaxies were spirals that looked like normal spiral galaxies at first, but when factoring in distance, turned out to be enormous.

Now that the super spirals have been discovered, scientists are working to discover how they have grown so large and why they haven't turned into elliptical galaxies. Typically, spiral galaxies reach a size limit when the gas they feed on to fuel star formation begins to move in so fast, it heats up and inhibits star formation. It may be that the super spirals are not the result of one continuously growing galaxy but the merger of two spiral galaxies. Yet galactic collisions between spiral galaxies typically disturb the relatively delicate spiral arms and form elliptical galaxies. How, then, did these super spiral galaxies remain spirals?

Scientists have two major methods for answering this question and other questions of galaxy formation and evolution. They can create simulations based on hypotheses for how formation works and see if the end result of the simulation looks like the observed distribution and structure of galaxies that we see today. They can also use telescopes and other instruments to observe the universe far back in time and gather as much detailed information as possible.

From a computer simulation perspective, simulating galaxy formation is a complex process. The starting point, the CMB, has relatively simple physics, and scientists can input data from Planck and other probes to represent the statistical properties of how the universe fluctuated in density and temperature at that time.

As the universe gets older, however, the physics get much more complicated. Different branches of physics start interacting, such as the nuclear and atomic physics within stars, radiation transport physics, and light moving through space and interacting with gas and matter. The equations required to model such physics are difficult to solve in a computer. Scientists would also like to incorporate more realistic physics such as the effects of stars forming and dying, and the effects of supernova energy on simulations, which currently pose large computational problems. As computers

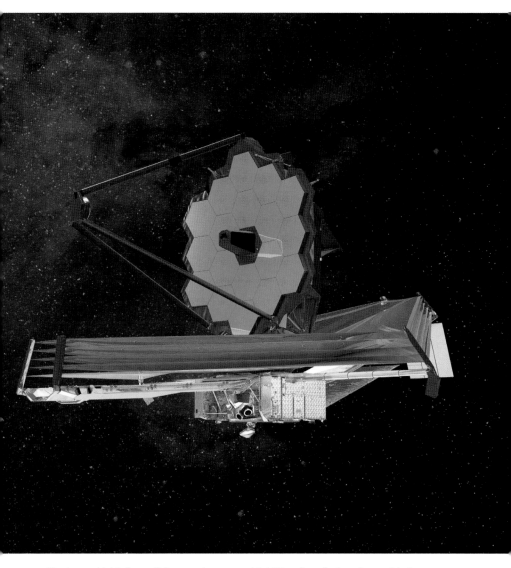

The James Webb Space Telescope has a sunshield the size of a tennis court to keep it cool.

get faster and larger, and as graphics processing cards improve, scientists hope that they will be able to make more robust and higher-fidelity simulations.

On the telescope front, NASA's James Webb Space Telescope (JWST) is one of the telescopes designed to hunt for detailed observations of galaxy formation. The JWST will also observe the evolution of galaxies from birth to present day, study star formation from birth to planetary systems, measure the properties of planetary systems, and search for the potential of life within those systems. To do so, the JWST will need to observe regions of space at least thirteen billion light years away from Earth so it can look back far enough in time and find the earliest galaxies and luminous objects.

Compared to the Hubble Space Telescope, the JWST has longer wavelength coverage and enhanced sensitivity, which will help it look further back in time and also see inside the dust clouds from which the first galaxies and stars formed.

The JWST is set to launch in October 2018.

MAPPING THE DARK SIDE

As understood in our current LCDM cosmology, dark matter and dark energy (Lambda) have a tremendous effect on galaxy structure and evolution. How can we learn more about these mysterious forces?

Dark Matter

One of the biggest questions in astrophysics today pertains to dark matter. While astronomers have been able to image and map the distribution of dark matter throughout the galaxy, we know little about what it actually is. Scientists think that it is not baryonic matter (which accounts for nearly all of the matter we encounter). Baryonic clouds absorb radiation, and dark matter does not. It is not antimatter (antimatter particles are identical to their corresponding particles but have the opposite spin and charge). When antimatter and matter meet, the antimatter annihilates matter, and the result produces gamma rays, which dark matter does not. They are not black holes, which we can tell based on patterns of gravitational lensing. It is currently believed that dark matter is some class of subatomic particle produced in the Big Bang and permeating space.

Because dark matter particles interact weakly, it is a challenge to detect and study them. The DAMA experiment group, one of the leaders in the hunt for dark matter, conducts their studies in the Gran Sasso laboratory east of Rome, buried in the mountains under 1400 meters of rock. The rock absorbs other sources of radiation and reduces background noise in the detector.

DAMA looks for flashes of light that theory suggests should occur when dark matter particles collide with sodium iodide crystals. DAMA first reported signs of dark matter particles in 1998. As they predicted, the flashes per day varied over time. No other experimental group has replicated DAMA's results, but up until 2016, no other group has

Particle interactions within xenon create light, and the sensitive light detectors can sense even a single photon.

used sodium iodide. That left the possibility that dark matter interacts uniquely with sodium iodide compared to other elements.

By 2016, other teams in the hunt for dark matter had sodium iodide detectors underway. The Korea Invisible Mass Search (KIMS) and DM-Ice (run from Yale University) have built a detector in South Korea at the Yangyang Underground Laboratory. The University of Zaragoza is building a detector at the Canfranc Underground Laboratory in the Spanish Pyrenees. The teams will share their data as they attempt to either prove or disprove the DAMA group's results. Another group out of Princeton is building two detectors, one at Gran Sasso and another in a gold mine in Victoria, Australia.

All of the above-mentioned groups use sodium iodide in their detectors. Another significant detection effort is the XENON experiment, which includes 120 scientists from twenty-two institutions around the world, including Columbia University, Purdue University, the University of California, Los Angeles (UCLA) and more. The XENON detectors, also located in the Gran Sasso laboratory in Italy, use stainless-steel tanks of liquid xenon gas. The tanks include sensors that can detect even single electrons and photons generated by dark matter passing through the liquid.

Other dark-matter detectors have been built across the world including in South Dakota, Canada, Japan, China, and another in the Gran Sasso laboratory.

Dark Energy

If we know little about dark matter, we know even less about dark energy. And yet, dark energy accounts for about 68 percent of the universe and is the force responsible for the increasing expansion of the universe.

It is possible that like space-time, dark energy is a property of space. The version of Einstein's theory of general relativity with a cosmological constant (lambda, often written as Λ) holds that additional space can come into existence and that space can possess its own energy. Einstein added Λ to force his equations to counteract gravity and produce a static universe. He discarded the constant when Hubble showed the universe was expanding.

Einstein thought the cosmological constant was his "greatest blunder" and regretted adding it to his equation. Today, however, some scientists think that the cosmological constant could represent the energy density of the vacuum that causes space to expand.

If the cosmological constant represents dark energy, it would require a new understanding of physics and the forces of nature. It is possible that Einstein's greatest mistake was actually one of his most incredible discoveries, even if he didn't know it at the time.

A new camera attached to the Blanco telescope in Chile called the Dark Energy Survey will study the behavior of dark energy, specifically the ratio of its pressure and energy density. The camera will also look for changes in matter distribution over time, which could show whether dark energy changes over time or whether gravity operates differently on large scales. Other telescopes on the hunt for dark energy measurements include the James Webb Space

Telescope and ground-based telescopes including the Giant Magellan Telescope and Large Synoptic Survey Telescope. The European Space Agency is currently building the technology for a satellite, the Euclid spacecraft, to search for dark energy. NASA is working on a new space observatory, Wide Field InfraRed Survey Telescope (WFIRST), partly to study dark energy as well as to make galactic and extragalactic surveys.

EFFECTS ON OUR DAILY LIVES

In some ways, our quest to learn more about the evolution of stars and galaxies is a practical matter. In the short term, searching for answers to far-off mysteries drives technological advancements and new knowledge that shape our earthly lives. By searching for more accurate laws of physics, Einstein created equations that changed the outcome of a war and shaped the lives of everyone on Earth. Sometimes, theoretical advancements have vast practical implications.

Beyond the scope of our own lifetime, astrophysics research also tells us more about the eventual death of our sun and the fate of our own galaxy. In about five billion years, the sun will die, first becoming a **red giant** that swallows Earth and then settling into a white dwarf.

Before the sun swallows Earth, however, a more dramatic event is predicted to unfold in our galactic neighborhood. In about four billion years, the Milky

Andromeda has a small companion galaxy, Triangulum, that will also collide with the Milky Way.

Way and Andromeda galaxies are expected to collide and merge into an elliptical galaxy. While the universe itself is expanding and the distance between far off galaxies is increasing, the gravitational attraction between the Milky Way and Andromeda is great enough that the two galaxies are moving toward each other, as evidenced by blue shifts in Andromeda's light. Scientists estimate that Andromeda is on a path headed toward the Milky Way at 402,000 kilometers per hour.

The distance between stars inside each galaxy is so great that very few, if any, will collide in the merger. Instead, the galaxies will hit and move through each other in a messy collision that will unfold over a billion years, whisking stars into new places. When it's settled, the stars from each galaxy will move in new orbits around the new galactic center. The sun, still alive, will likely be moved to the outskirts of the new elliptical galaxy.

The collision is expected to take place at a point when the sun is so hot that (at least Earth-based) humans are unlikely to be around to see it happen. If humanity is around, somewhere, though, scientists predict the event will include a beautiful, billion-year-long light show.

Somewhere in between the potential application of space technology and information to Earth-based pursuits and the final death throes of our sun lies another application of our discoveries: they teach us about who we are today and where we are going.

Several hundred years ago, the brightest, most educated people believed that Earth was at the center of the universe and that the stars were fixed in the sky. At the turn of the twentieth century, scientists still believed that the Milky Way was the only galaxy in the universe. Such conceptions of the universe make it easy to place our species and our planet on a pedestal. Surely we are the most important beings in the cosmos. Surely the point of the universe is our existence.

Such beliefs are harder to support when we know that we are but a small planet revolving around a small star on the edge of a very ordinary galaxy. We must instead ask: What else is out there? Who else is out there? Is there a viable place for humanity to move if we strip this planet of the resources that sustain us?

As we face the realities of global warming, habitat destruction, resource depletion, and more, we are at a point where today's scientists are looking at how to move from life on Earth to life in space. The entrepreneur Elon Musk founded SpaceX to build space technology that can someday enable people to live on other planets. The tech giant Amazon funds a company, Blue Origin, dedicated to reducing the cost and improving the safety of sending ordinary humans to live and work in space. As some scientists work to understand more about the universe, many others are working to expand our presence within it.

Science and technology have always transported humans through great leaps forward. We research the unknown to make those leaps possible.

Glossary

baryonic In astronomy, the type of matter composed of protons, neutrons, and electrons, also called normal atomic matter. Stars, planets, and gas clouds are baryonic.

binary star A star system of two stars orbiting around their common center of mass, estimated to be roughly half of the stars in the sky.

black hole A region of space in which gravity is so strong that no matter or light can escape.

cosmic microwave background The thermal radiation that remained after the Big Bang. Today, the CMB is very cold but still observable in the microwave portion of the electromagnetic spectrum.

dark energy An unknown force believed to be responsible for the accelerating expansion of the universe; dark energy makes up approximately 68 percent of the universe.

dark matter Matter that does not absorb, reflect, or emit light that we can detect through its gravitational effects on galaxy structure. Dark matter makes up approximately 27 percent of the universe, and 85 percent of total matter in the universe.

event horizon The boundary around a black hole after which no light or other radiation can escape.

galaxy A system of stars, along with gas and dust, bound together by gravity. The Sun is a star in the Milky Way galaxy.

gravitational lensing The distortion and bending of light due to gravity.

interstellar medium The matter that fills the space between stars, which has a very low density of gas and dust.

Jeans instability The gravitational instability that occurs when the internal gas pressure of an interstellar gas cloud is not strong enough to prevent gravitational collapse, leading to star formation.

Kelvin scale A scale of temperature where 0 equals absolute zero, or the point where all molecular movement stops. Like Celsius, the difference between water's freezing point and boiling point is 100 degrees, which means one Kelvin degree has the same magnitude as one Celsius degree.

luminosity The intrinsic brightness of an object, or the amount of light emitted from an object's surface; in contrast to apparent brightness (how bright an object appears), which depends on distance.

nebula An interstellar cloud of gas and dust, originally used as the name for any luminous, diffuse objects, including other galaxies.

neutron star The very compact and dense remnant of a massive star after supernova.

parsec A distance equal to 3.26 light years, often expressed in kiloparsecs (1000 parsecs) or megaparsecs (1,000,000 parsecs).

plasma An ionized gas with essentially no electric charge that occurs in conditions with low pressure or very high temperatures.

quantum theory A theory of matter and energy based on quantum mechanics, or the laws that govern the tiniest particles including atoms and electrons.

quasar An extremely massive and remote celestial object that releases a huge amount of light, thought to be powered by the accretion of material into a supermassive black hole.

red giant A late stage of stellar evolution in which the star expands and becomes more luminous and, due to a lower surface temperature, emits red light.

redshift A shift of emission and absorption lines toward the red end of the electromagnetic spectrum that occurs when an object in space is moving away from the observer.

spectrograph An instrument that separates and measures the wavelength of electromagnetic radiation so that it can be recorded and analyzed.

supernova A large explosion in which a star ejects most of its mass, sending gas and debris into space.

Further Information

Books

Frebel, Anna. *Searching for the Oldest Stars: Ancient Relics from the Early Universe.* Princeton, NJ: Princeton University Press, 2015.

Hawking, Stephen. *A Brief History of Time.* New York: Bantam Books, 2011.

Lang, Kenneth R. *The Life and Death of Stars.* New York: Cambridge University Press, 2013.

Sagan, Carl. *Cosmos.* New York: Ballantine Books, 2013.

Websites

Explore the Universe
http://www.airandspace.si.edu/exhibitions/explore-the-universe/online/etu_ne.htm
Take a tour of the instruments scientists have used to study the universe over time, from the naked eye to spectrographs to wide-field cameras. *Explore the Universe* is an online version of the Smithsonian exhibit of the same name.

Hubble Space Telescope

http://www.nasa.gov/mission_pages/hubble/main/index.html

Learn about the Hubble Space Telescope mission, see tweets and photos of the day, and explore images taken from the Hubble's adventures through space.

Videos

A Virtual Universe

http://www.youtube.com/watch?v=SY0bKE10ZDM

Watch a simulation of the evolution of the universe created by scientists from the Massachusetts Institute of Technology and learn how this simulation was built.

Dark Energy and the Runaway Universe

http://www.youtube.com/watch?v=Guvv5olLxCQ

The only astrophysicist on both of the teams that won the Nobel Prize for discovering the accelerating expansion of the universe talks about how the discovery happened.

Bibliography

"Assembly of Galaxies." James Webb Space Telescope. Retrieved April 28, 2016. http://www.jwst.nasa.gov/galaxies.html

Bartusiak, Marcia. *Black Hole: How an Idea Abandoned by Newtonians, Hated by Einstein, and Gambled on by Hawking Became Loved.* New Haven, CT: Yale University Press, 2015.

Chaisson, Eric J. "Cosmic Evolution from Big Bang to Humankind." *Harvard College Observatory* last modified 2013. http://www.cfa.harvard.edu/~ejchaisson/cosmic_evolution/docs/splash.html

"DAMA Experiment." *Gran Sasso National Laboratory.* September 9, 2013. Retrieved on April 27, 2016. http://www. lngs.infn.it/lngs_infn/contents/lngs_en/public/educational/physics/experiments/current/dama/

Frost, Robert. "Desert Places" in *A Further Range.* New York, NY: Henry Holt & Co, 1936.

Garner, Rob, Ed. "About the Hubble Space Telescope." *NASA* last modified April 11, 2016. http://www.nasa.gov/mission_pages/hubble/story/index.html

"Hayden Planetarium." *placeMatters*. Retrieved on April 27, 2016. http://www.placematters.net/node/1781

Hawking, Stephen. *Stephen Hawking on Black Holes*. Video. November 18, 2013. http://www.youtube.com/watch?v=K1CefSyt-bs

Loeb, Abraham. *How Did the First Stars and Galaxies Form?* Princeton, NJ: Princeton University Press, 2010.

Panek, Richard. "The Father of Dark Matter Still Gets No Respect." *Discover Magazine*. January 2009.

Perlmutter, Saul. "Exploring Supernovae Leads to Physics Nobel Prize." Interview with *Fresh Air*. November 14, 2011. http://www.npr.org/2011/11/14/142248148/exploring-supernovas-leads-to-physics-nobel-prize

Sagan, Carl. *Cosmos*. New York, NY: Ballantine Books, 2013.

Thorne, Kip. *Black Holes and Time Warps: Einstein's Outrageous Legacy*. New York, NY: W. W. Norton & Company, 1994.

Treu, Tommaso. "History of the Universe." Lecture 13 slides from Astro-2 at the University of California, Santa Barbara, May 30, 2013. Retrieved April 27, 2016. http://web.physics.ucsb.edu/~tt/ASTRO2/lecture13.pdf

Index

Page numbers in **boldface** are illustrations. Entries in **boldface** are glossary terms.

About the Author

Rachel Keranen is a writer based in Madison, Wisconsin. Her work focuses on science, software, and entrepreneurship. She's passionate about learning and loves taking deep dives into science and history. In addition to the books that she writes, Keranen's previous work includes articles in the *Minneapolis/St. Paul Business Journal* and *London Business Matters* magazine.

Keranen enjoys traveling, biking, and spending time near water. As a young girl, her parents often pulled her out of bed in the middle of the night to watch shooting stars and meteor showers.